THE FIVE TRUTHS ABOUT WORK-LIFE BALANCE

JAE ELLARD

There is no need for a long, wordy introduction to set up the intention of this book.

This book is about the myths and misconceptions surrounding the many interconnected roles, relationships, and responsibilities we face each day, often referred to as this thing called "work-life balance."

WHEN IT COMES TO
THIS THING CALLED
WORK-LIFE BALANCE, - - - - - - - -

THERE ARE
FIVE TRUTHS
TO KNOW.

THE
FIRST
TRUTH

YOU CAN DEFINE
WORK-LIFE BALANCE
HOWEVER YOU WANT.

There are a lot of ways to talk about this concept, but only one way that feels right for you.

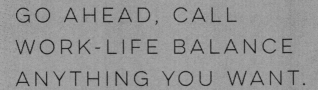

GO AHEAD, CALL WORK-LIFE BALANCE ANYTHING YOU WANT.

work-life *balance*

work-life *harmony*

work-life *awareness*

work-life *integration*

work-life *flexibility*

work-life *flow*

work-life _____
(fill in the blank)

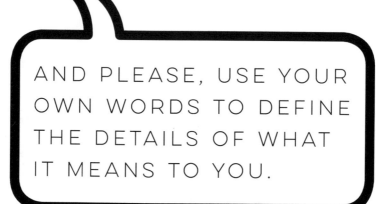

AND PLEASE, USE YOUR OWN WORDS TO DEFINE THE DETAILS OF WHAT IT MEANS TO YOU.

calm

free of guilt

composed

flexibility

harmony

distraction-free days and nights

sense of equilibrium

serene in body and mind

engaged

present

in alignment

happy

satisfied with choices

in the moment

peaceful

freedom

fulfilled

Most people share a similar desire, which is to create easy joy and meaningful engagement between the interconnected roles, relationships, and responsibilities that make up life.

That said, there are as many ways as there are people on the planet to describe what living a balanced life would feel like.

When it comes to balance,
everybody has their own idea of what is

COMFORTABLE,

TOLERABLE,

AND

ACCEPTABLE.

THERE IS NO RIGHT
OR WRONG WAY TO
DEFINE BALANCE.
IT IS WHAT IT IS
FOR YOU AND FOR
YOU ALONE.

THE
SECOND
TRUTH

YOU WILL BE IN AND
OUT OF BALANCE
YOUR ENTIRE LIFE.

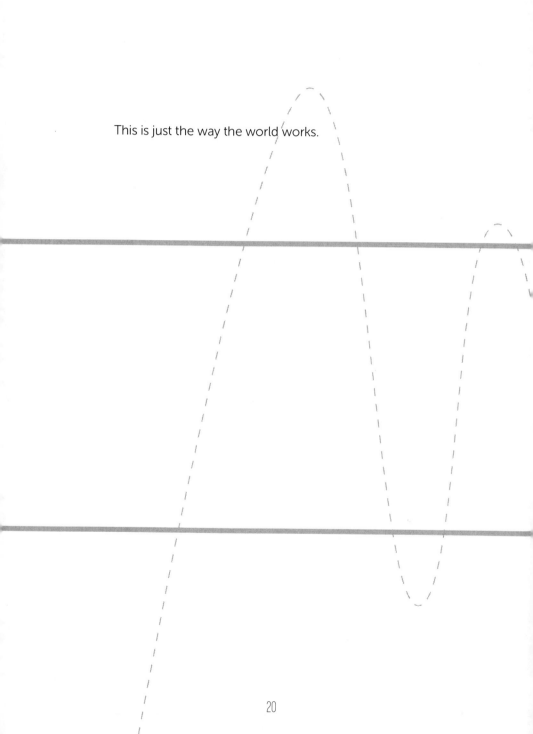

This is just the way the world works.

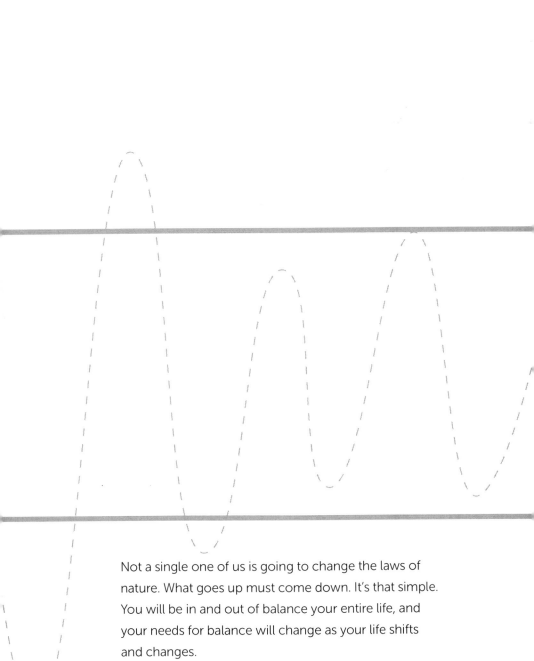

Not a single one of us is going to change the laws of
nature. What goes up must come down. It's that simple.
You will be in and out of balance your entire life, and
your needs for balance will change as your life shifts
and changes.

Things like new jobs, new relationships, new homes, new roles, new hobbies, births, deaths, and health (yours and others') will all impact your needs for balance.

YOUR NEEDS FOR
BALANCE WILL
FOREVER BE EVOLVING.

Your secret power is in recognizing and accepting that what you need now, in this moment, is very different than what you will need 12 months from now or one, five, seven, or 10 years from now.

Once you have accepted that your needs will change, it becomes about knowing and understanding your needs, making choices that support your needs, and communicating your needs with the important people in your life.

YOU WILL BE IN AND OUT OF BALANCE YOUR ENTIRE LIFE. ACKNOWLEDGING AND ACCEPTING ACCOUNTABILITY FOR YOUR NEEDS, WANTS, AND DESIRES IS YOUR SECRET POWER.

THE
THIRD
TRUTH

WORK-LIFE BALANCE HAS NOTHING TO DO WITH WORK.

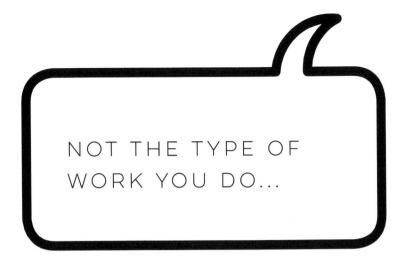

NOT THE TYPE OF
WORK YOU DO...

the level you are at,

the hours you put in,

the hours you feel like you
should be putting in,

or even if the job you have is not paid,

like being a student,

a volunteer,

raising children,

or running a household.

We all have responsibilities that can be considered work. Whether you get paid for what you do or not.

More than that, balance has nothing to do with your gender, family structure, parental status, religion, education, income, or geographic location.

Work-life balance is not about any of these things specifically — it's mostly about the type of conversations we have or the conversations we avoid having about these things, as well as our feelings about the impact of these things on our lives.

Most of the issues we attribute to being "out of balance" at work or at home can be traced back to (and resolved through) a conversation – to be specific, an authentic conversation. (You know, the kind where you say what you REALLY mean.)

What gets us in trouble and keeps us busy and disengaged are the conversations we are NOT having with our boss, our business partners, our customers, our friends, our significant others, our children, and – especially – ourselves.

It's possible that 99% of the time, these conversations we are not having are about the triggers that are causing the imbalance in our life.

These triggers, most times, boil down to your values and the boundaries (or lack of boundaries) that support and honor your values in all the relationships you are in.

THE RELATIONSHIP
YOU HAVE WITH WORK,

RELATIONSHIPS YOU
HAVE WITH OTHERS
(IN AND OUT OF WORK),

AND THE RELATIONSHIP
YOU HAVE WITH YOURSELF.

Why are so many people not having these types of conversations?

The answer is simple. In most cases, it boils down to fear: Fear of rejection. Fear of being perceived as "less than." Fear of failing. Fear of asking for help. Fear of being different. Fear of actually being perceived as both balanced and successful.

Sometimes these conversations that we avoid are about saying no (and our fear of saying no).

NO

Saying no to someone at work or someone you love might let them down, and no one wants to let anyone down, especially on purpose.

Let's be honest: It's easier to say no to your own needs than to disappoint someone else. (Even if it means disappointing yourself.)

When you say yes to people, requests, and projects, that are in conflict with your values, or when you engage with people who do not support – or even worse, who disrespect – your values, you are actually saying "no" to yourself and creating imbalance in your life.

WORK-LIFE BALANCE HAS NOTHING TO DO WITH WORK. IT'S ABOUT AUTHENTICALLY OWNING AND CLEARLY COMMUNICATING YOUR YES'S AND NO'S TO THE PEOPLE WHO SHARE YOUR LIFE (WHICH INCLUDES YOURSELF).

THE
FOURTH
TRUTH

CREATING BALANCE
IS FREE.

(GREAT NEWS – BECAUSE
EVERYONE LOVES FREE!)

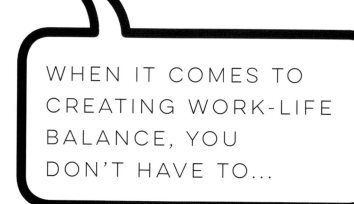

WHEN IT COMES TO CREATING WORK-LIFE BALANCE, YOU DON'T HAVE TO...

quit your job

hire a nanny

eat more vegetables

sleep more

give up sweets

stop going online

find new friends

examine your relationship
with your mobile phone

join a gym

find a therapist

hire a professional coach

acquire advanced degrees
or certifications

meditate

join a support group

read self-help books

wait until the kids go to college

change your routine

These are all options you can choose – but you don't have to do any of them.

The only thing you have to do is

CHOOSE

balance as a lifestyle.

Okay, so you make the choice – you want balance. Then what?

START SMALL.

PAY ATTENTION MORE.

Yes, really.

PAY ATTENTION.

Many people don't spend much time where they are. They are either still thinking about where they have been or thinking about where they will be – which robs them of being *where* they are *when* they are there.

The richest of the rich and the poorest of the poor have equal access to the currency of presence.

There is no cost whatsoever to being present.

It's F R E E to pay attention to your environment and see and feel as much (or as little) of the experience that you want.

It's F R E E to pay attention to the people and the relationships in your life – to slow down, to really hear what is being said, and to notice what is not being said.

It's F R E E to pay attention to you. Your body, your feelings, your wants, your desires, and especially, your thoughts.

We have all experienced this thing called presenteeism.

This is when you show up physically, but not mentally. The impact is that you are unable to be in the moment and contribute your best, because you are distracted about whatever might happen in the future or are reliving what has happened in the past.

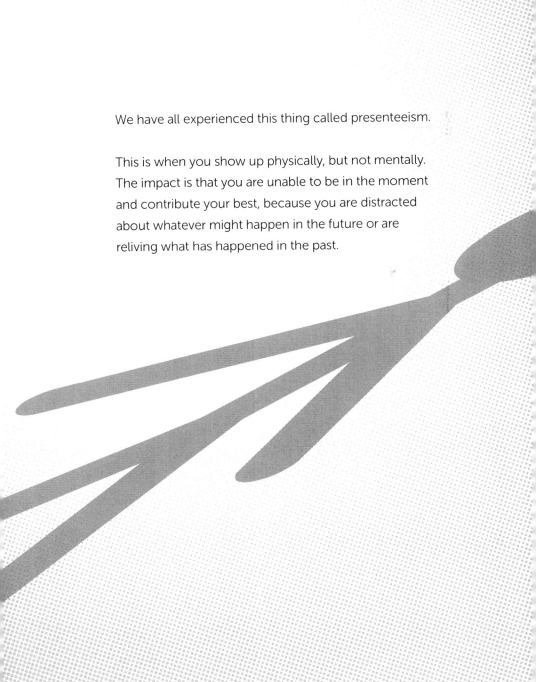

(It's okay — we've all done it, and will do it again,
because sometimes that's just what happens.)

Odds are you already have a pretty great life. Paying more attention might make it feel even better.

Connecting to what you already have is free. It's the disconnection that can cost you dearly.

CREATING BALANCE
IS FREE. AND IT CAN
BEGIN RIGHT THIS
MOMENT.

THE
FIFTH
TRUTH

THE CHOICE IS
YOURS TO CREATE
BALANCE EACH DAY.

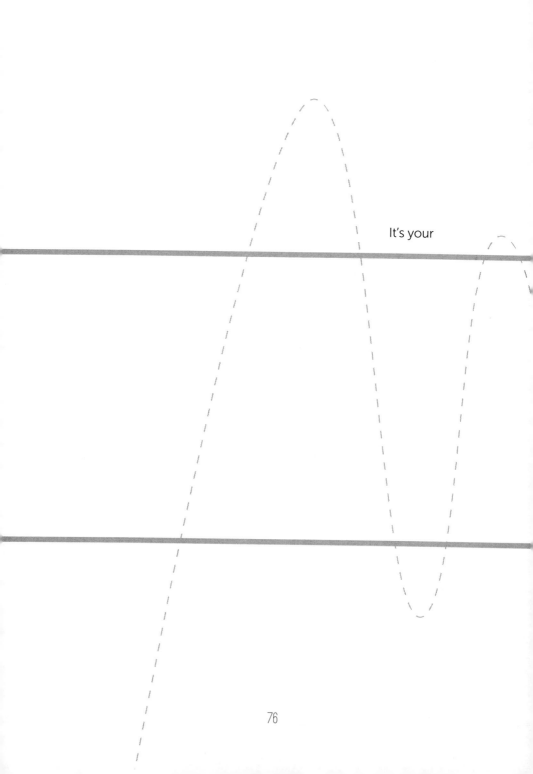

It's your

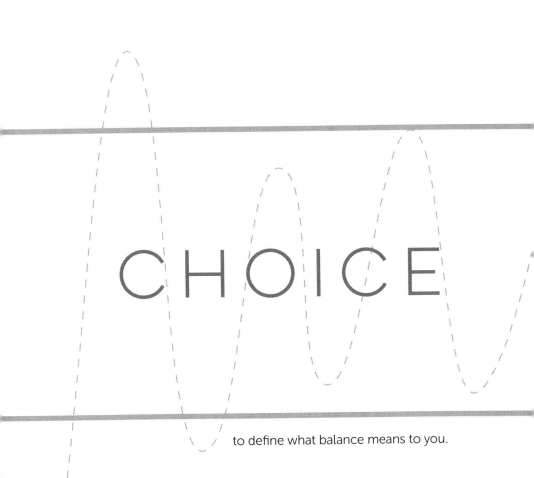

CHOICE

to define what balance means to you.

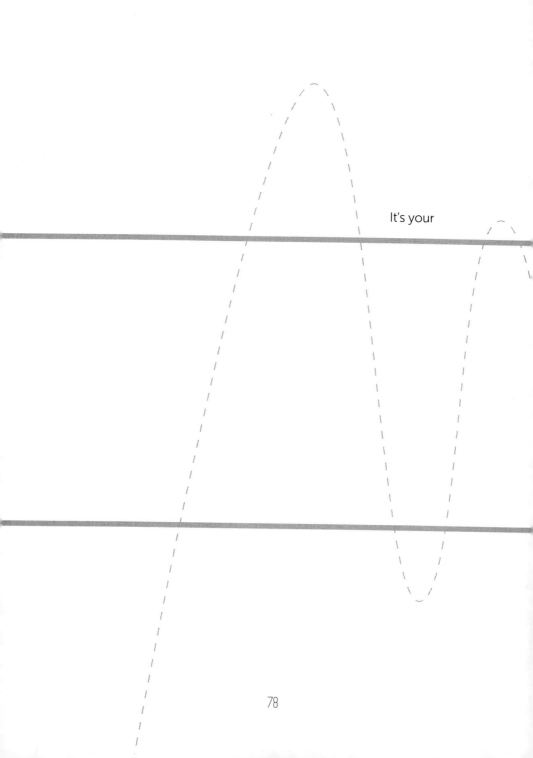

It's your

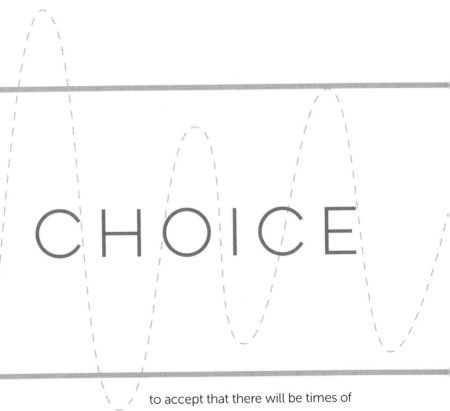

CHOICE

to accept that there will be times of greater imbalance.

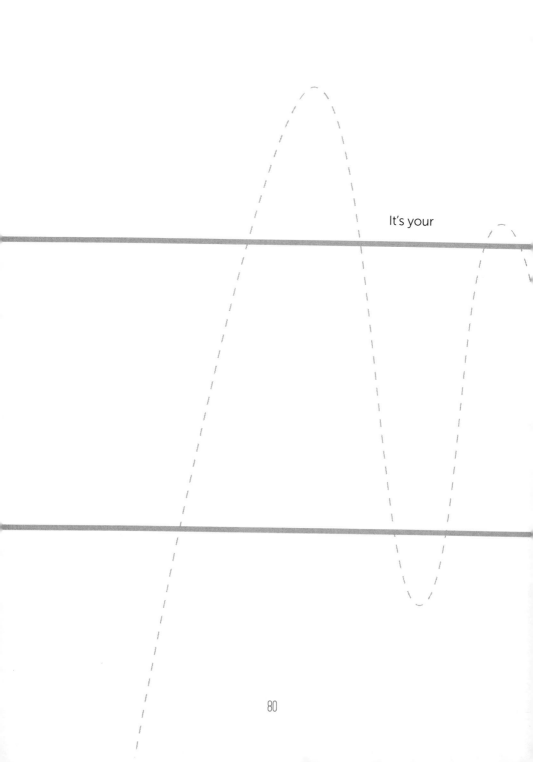

It's your

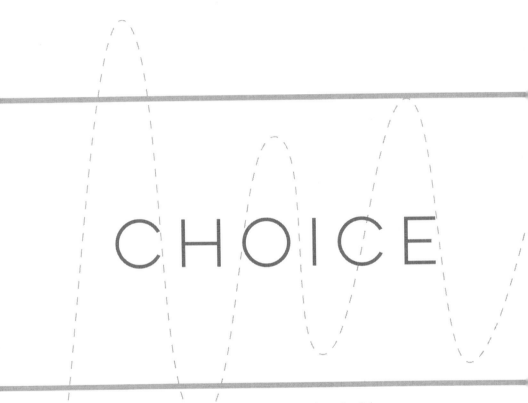

CHOICE

to own and authentically express your yes's and no's.

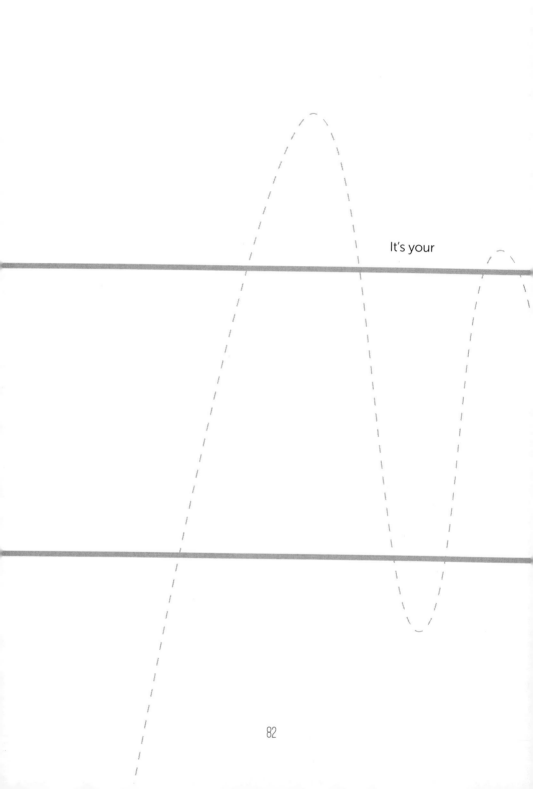

It's your

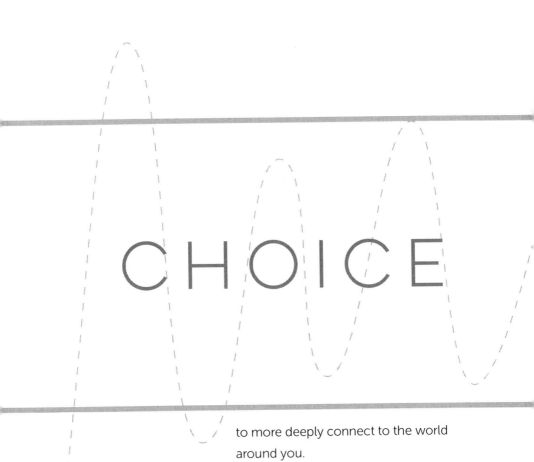

CHOICE

to more deeply connect to the world around you.

Some days you might make choices that support your definition of balance, and other days you might make choices that sabotage the type of balance you are seeking.

The magic is that every single day, the choice is yours to make

AGAIN,

AGAIN, AND

AGAIN.

THE FIVE TRUTHS ABOUT WORK-LIFE BALANCE ARE SIMPLE:

1 You can define work-life balance however you want.

2 You will be in and out of balance your entire life.

3 Balance has nothing to do with work.

4 Creating balance is free.

5 The choice is yours to create balance each day.

WHAT YOU CHOOSE TO
DO WITH THESE TRUTHS
IS UP TO YOU.

THE CHOICE IS YOURS.

ABOUT THE AUTHOR

In 2008, Jae Ellard founded Simple Intentions, a company dedicated to developing employee awareness and publishing conscious content. In 2010, Jae authored the Mindful Life Program designed to help people disrupt patterns that cause imbalance and disengagement. To date, Jae's work has touched thousands of employees at multinational corporations in more than 50 countries spanning from Asia Pacific to Latin American, Western and Central Europe, Middle East, as well as Canada the United States. Jae has an extensive background in writing and communication with a master's degree in Communication Management from Colorado State University and a bachelor's degree in Broadcast Communication from Metropolitan State College of Denver. As a lifelong learner her passion has propelled her deep into research on human behavior, neuroscience, mindfulness, and organizational relationship systems. Jae writes columns and speaks on mindfulness in the workplace and is the author of seven books.

OTHER BOOKS BY JAE ELLARD

The Pocket Coach: Perspective When You Need Some is a book of questions to help you make clear choices.

Success with Stress is about five proactive choices you can make to reduce stress.

THE MINDFUL LIFE COLLECTION

STOP & Think: Creating New Awareness is about the choices you have and the understanding of the impact of the choices you make.

STOP & See: Developing Intentional Habits is about your ability to consciously choose to create habits that support your definitions of balance and success.

STOP & Listen: Practicing Presence is about working with your choices to create deeper engagement with self, others, and your environment.

Beyond Tips & Tricks: Mindful Management is about leading groups to take accountability for making and accepting choices.

Written by Jae Ellard

Edited by Jenifer Kooiman

Designed by Hannah Wygal

ISBN-13: 978-0986238703

ISBN-10: 0986238708

The Five Truths about Work-Life Balance, 1st edition

2014 Copyright by Simple Intentions Inc.

This book may be ordered directly through the publisher at www.simpleintentions.com.

Contact: Simple Intentions, Inc., www.simpleintentions.com.

Simple Intentions creates conscious content to generate intentional conversations.

Made in the USA
San Bernardino, CA
03 March 2015